One-Minute Math
Developmental Drill
Level A Addition
Sums 0 to 10

Author: Theresa Warnick
Cover Artist: Good Neighbor Press

Frank Schaffer Publications®

Send all inquiries to:
Frank Schaffer Publications
3195 Wilson Drive NW
Grand Rapids, Michigan 49544

ISBN 0-7647-0391-9

5 6 7 8 9 10 11   09 08 07 06 05

Directions for Use

Setting up the Program

Reproduce enough copies of the tests for the class. You may wish to separate the tests by fact into file folders and organize the folders in a storage box. This provides handy access to the tests and a quick view of the pages which need to be replenished.

Using a manila file folder for each student offers easy organization and provides a simple method of distributing the daily tests.

Using the Flash Cards

A set of flash cards is required for each student. These serve as additional facilitators in learning and retaining basic math facts.

When beginning the program, give each student only those facts he or she has mastered on the progress chart <u>and</u> the first unchecked fact. This card will correspond to the test the student will be taking. Each time another fact is mastered, give the student the card for the next fact. When starting at the Zero Rule, the student should be given all the zero flash cards. You may wish to present this rule as: zero plus any number gives that number. When he or she progresses to the One Rule, the student is given all the one plus flash cards. The One Rule may be presented as: one plus any number gives the next number. After this point, the student will receive one flash card at a time. Unmastered flash cards may be left in the student's folder for easy access.

Encourage the use of the flash cards at home as well as at school. Depending on the number of cards being reviewed, you may wish to spend five to fifteen minutes a day on flash card practice.

Using the Bulletin Boards

The **"Shoot for the Stars"** bulletin board theme can be used to highlight the particular fact on which each student is working. Using the reproducible art found on pages vii-ix, write the math facts on the stars and write the students' names on the spaceships. Group their names around the particular fact on which they are working; when a fact is mastered, move that student's name card to the next fact star.

The **"Shoot for the Stars"** theme continues on the following reproducible pages: Manipulative Mat (xi), Activity Page (xiii), Games (xv-xvii), Awards (xviii), Certificates (xx) and Student Progress Chart (xxiii).

You may wish to change the bulletin board theme as students progress through the program. For the **"Climb Our Math Fact Tree"** theme, use the reproducible art found on page x. Write the students' names on the leaves and the facts to be learned on the branches. This theme also continues on the following reproducible pages: Manipulative Mat (xii), Activity Page (xiv), Awards (xix), and Certificates (xxi).

Using the Progress Charts

The progress chart shows the addition facts and indicates the scope and sequence of Level A (sums zero to ten). By checking off each fact a student masters, you can record each student's progress. Each student may track his or her own progress by coloring a copy of the personal progress chart found in the reproducible pages.

The Letter to Parents

The letter provided will help make parents aware of the objectives, components and methods of the One-Minute Math Developmental Drill series.

Awards and Certificate of Achievement

When a student completes a designated number of facts, you may wish to present him or her with an award found in the reproducible pages. The certificate may be used when all of the facts in the series are mastered.

Using the Manipulative Mats

It is important that students develop a good understanding of numbers. The following activities will help students create relations for numbers and will help strengthen their number sense.

Have the students work with a variety of materials on the manipulative mats (pages xi-xii). These mats may be laminated for extended use.

1. The mat is divided into two parts. Select a number of counters representing sums of ten or less. If, for example, the selected sum is five, the student may separate the counters on the mat into the following sets: 2+3, 3+2, 1+4, 4+1, 5+0, 0+5. Next, the student should verbalize the parts shown, for example: "Two plus three equals five." Allow the students adequate practice in manipulating the counters into sets showing all possible parts of a given sum.

2. Students should continue working with their manipulative mats and counters. On copies of activity pages xii-xiv, have the student draw the parts for a selected sum, and write its corresponding addition sentence.

3. Select a sum and ask the students to place the correct number of counters on their mats. Have the students write that number at the top of a blank sheet of paper. Students should use their counters to find all the possible combinations of parts for the sum and record them.

iii

4. Have the students work with partners. Select a sum from zero to ten. One student should divide the counters on the mat and cover one side of the mat. In the example, if the sum is know to be five, the student's partner must answer the question, "Three and what number make five?" Continue this activity with all sums of ten or less.

Using the Game Sheets

Game Sheet 1: Fill in the blank spaces on the path with the number facts you wish to reinforce. Using a gameboard spinner, the student moves ahead the number of spaces shown and must correctly answer the number fact to remain on that space. If the correct answer is given, the next player may take a turn. If the student answers incorrectly, he or she returns to the previously held space.

Game Sheet 2: Attach page A to page B. A student advances the game piece by dropping a marker, (coin, button, etc.) onto the center of the playing board. (If the marker does not land on any fact, the student forfeits his or her turn.) The student must answer the math fact or facts the marker is touching and may move the game piece ahead the number of correct answers given. For example: If the marker is touching two facts and the student answers only one correctly, the student may advance the game piece one space.

The games (sheets 1 and 2) may end when one player reaches the final space on the path or continue until all players reach the end space. Students may also play in teams. The first students to complete Game Sheet 1 may fill in the facts for the next game to be played.

Using the Timed Tests

Level A Addition teaches sums zero to ten. Each sheet contains 30 problems. There is a pretest and posttest for placement and evaluation. The particular fact the student is learning appears 40% of the time (twelve problems) on each test. The last previous fact mastered occurs 10% to 20% of the time (three to six problems). The remaining 40% to 50% of the problems on each sheet are those previously learned by the student, except for those pages labeled as tests, which usually present each fact only once.

An addition fact such as 3+7 is also presented as 7+3 on each page because of it commutative property.

Each student should complete a timed test every day if possible, starting with the lowest fact on the progress chart for that student. Remind the students to note the fact written in the upper left-hand corner, which indicates the fact on which they are working. Students must complete all the problems on a sheet accurately in one minute before advancing to the next fact. If the student has not completely and accurately answered all the problems when the minute has elapsed, he or she must complete a test for the same fact the next day. Alternate tests A and B until mastery is achieved.

If a student can pass the Zero Rule test, he or she has demonstrated the hand dexterity needed to complete the page in one minute. However, if students have extreme difficulty passing each fact page, you may wish to lengthen the amount of time allowed to complete the page by five or ten seconds.

It is important to allow students to see their progress on the same fact. All attempted tests may be left in the folder and the same fact test added on top for the next day. Students will become more proficient each time they are retested on the same fact until they finally master it.

Not all students will complete the entire program, but they will possess a greater proficiency of the facts they have mastered. Mastery, rather than completion, is the goal of the program.

Dear Parent,

In order to develop a good mathematics foundation, it is important that your child learn basic addition and subtraction facts. The <u>One-Minute Math Developmental Drill</u> program enables children to achieve this goal. The idea behind this program is that children must master a particular math fact before they are introduced to a new fact.

A flash card will be sent home each time your child begins learning a new addition fact. The flash cards will help your child memorize these facts more readily. Please have your child practice daily with <u>all</u> of the flash cards you have received. He or she should work toward answering each card in less than two seconds. Help your child with this activity if possible. Since it may take several days to commit some facts to memory, be patient with your child. Children will not learn all facts at the same rate. Do not expect your child to bring home a new flash card every day.

The Level A Addition program includes:

1. Pretest and posttest for placement and evaluation

2. 36 individual fact tests on sums zero to ten

    a. Each test contains 30 problems

    b. The particular fact a student is learning is covered in 40% of the test

    c. The previously learned fact is covered in 10% to 20% of the test

3. 36 flash cards for practicing the selected facts

4. Certificate upon completion

Thank you for working with me on this program.
Please contact me if you have any questions or concerns.

Sincerely,

Bulletin Board Themes

Shoot for the Stars

Climb Our Math Fact Tree

 FS-23241 One-Minute Math Level A Addition

Reproducible Art
Shoot for the Stars

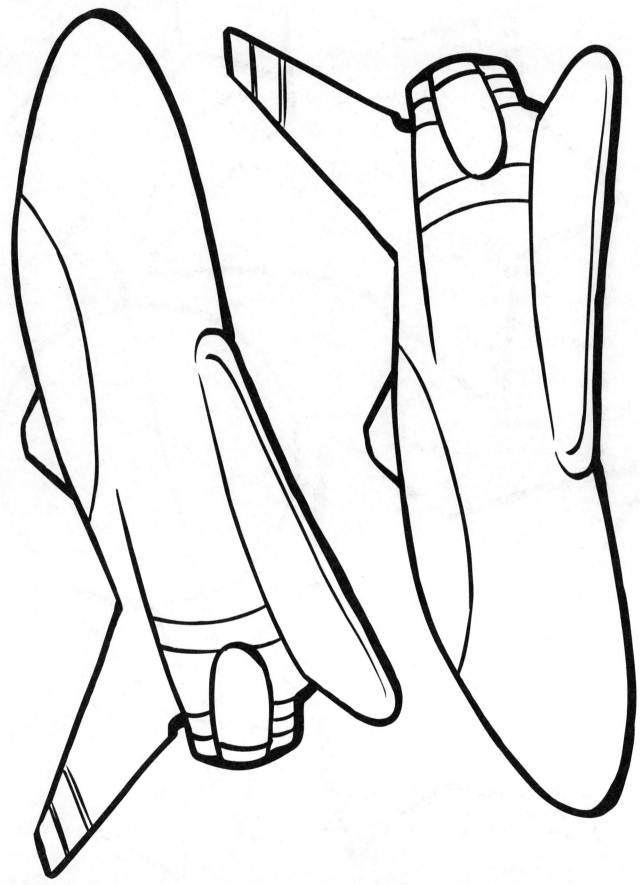

FS-23241 One-Minute Math Level A Addition

Reproducible Art
Shoot for the Stars

FS-23241 One-Minute Math Level A Addition

Reproducible Art
Shoot for the Stars

ix

Reproducible Art
Climb Our Math Fact Tree

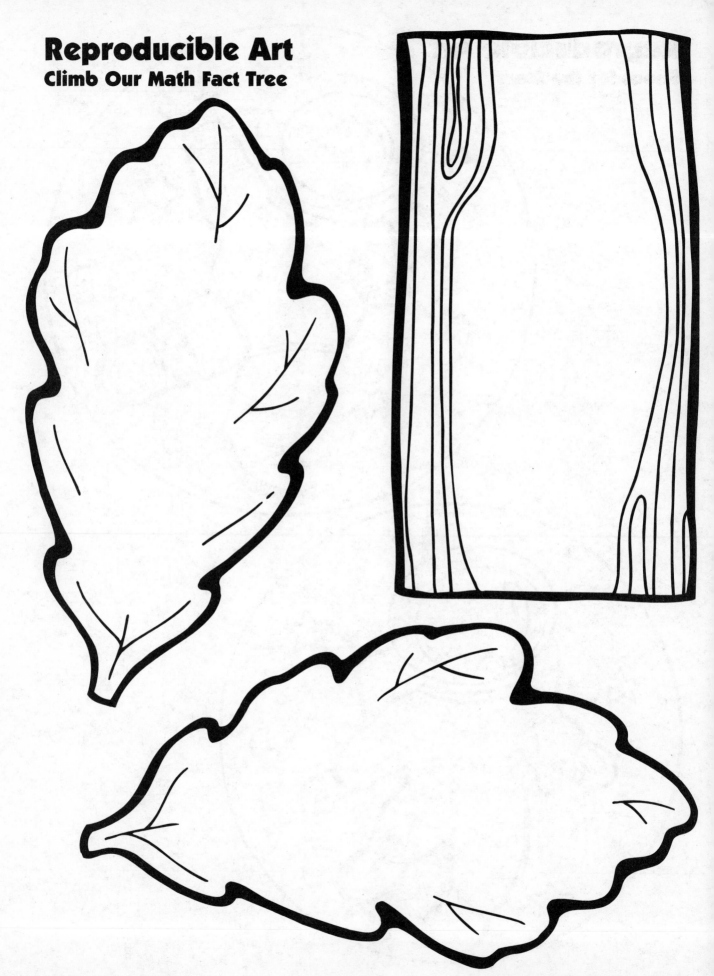

X FS-23241 One-Minute Math Level A Addition

Manipulative Mat
Shoot for the Stars

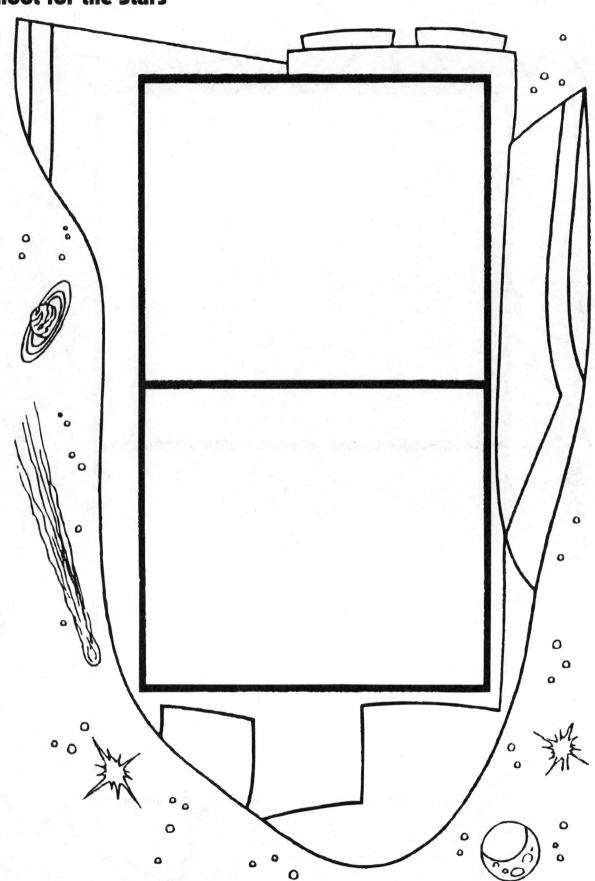

FS-23241 One-Minute Math Level A Addition

Manipulative Mat
Climb Our Math Fact Tree

FS-23241 One-Minute Math Level A Addition

Activity Page
Shoot for the Stars

Name _____

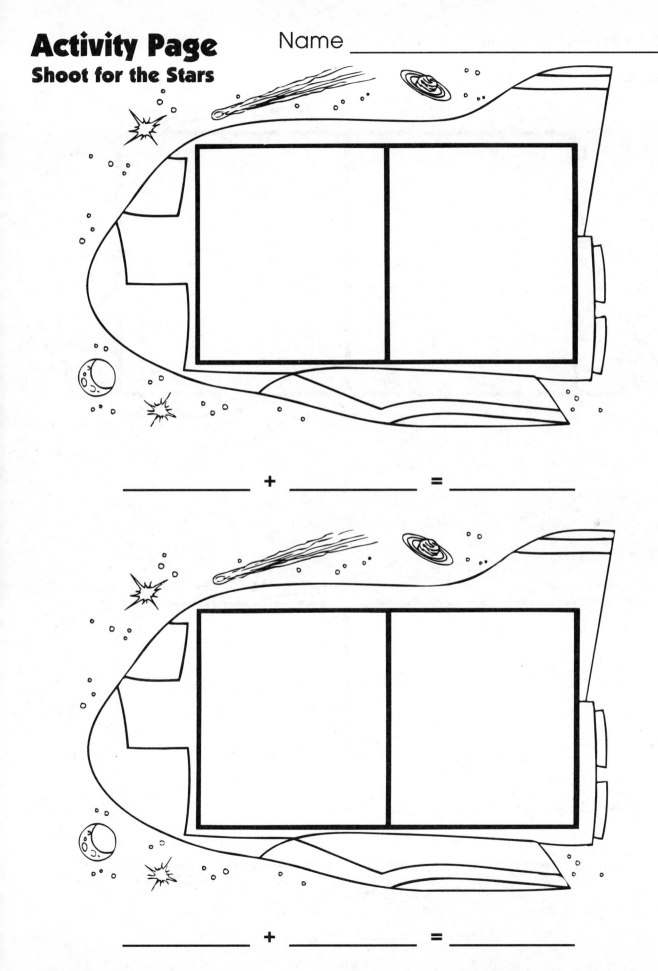

_____ + _____ = _____

_____ + _____ = _____

FS-23241 One-Minute Math Level A Addition

Activity Page
Climb Our Math Fact Tree

Name _____

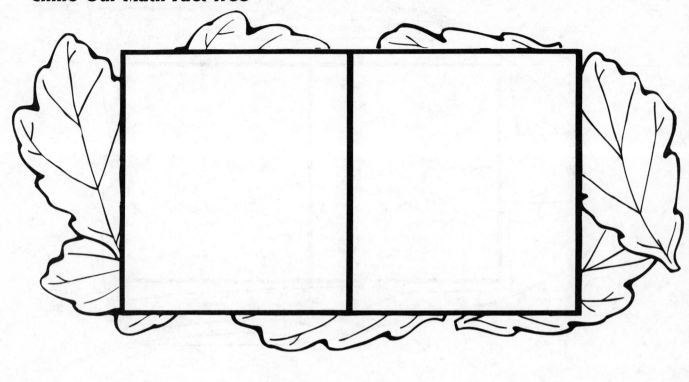

_____ + _____ = _____

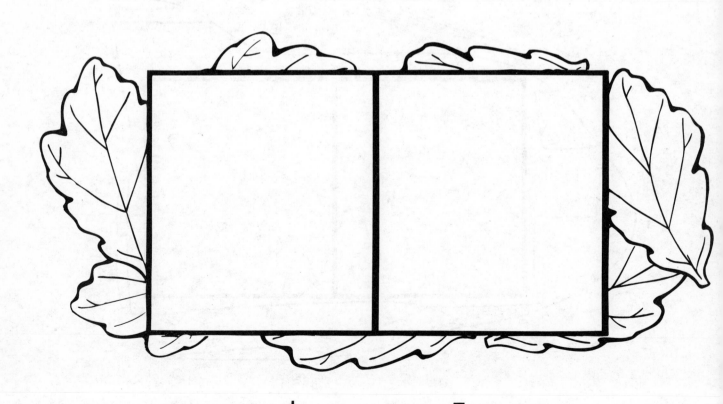

_____ + _____ = _____

        FS-23241 One-Minute Math Level A Addition

Game Sheet 1

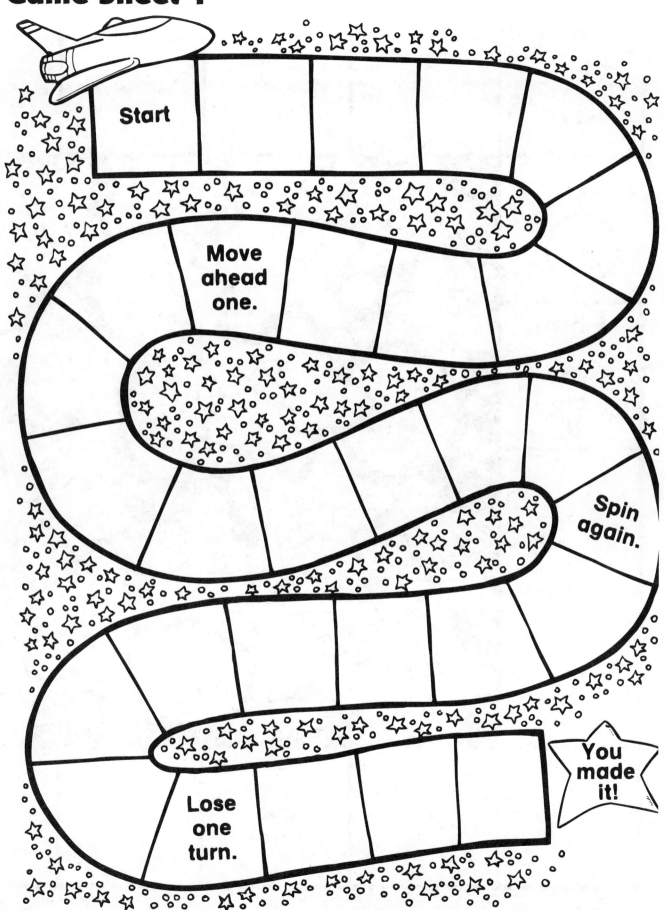

Start

Move ahead one.

Spin again.

Lose one turn.

You made it!

FS-23241 One-Minute Math Level A Addition

Game Sheet 2

Start

Finish

You did it!

$$\begin{array}{r} 5 \\ +5 \\ \hline \end{array}$$

$$\begin{array}{r} 7 \\ +1 \\ \hline \end{array}$$

$$\begin{array}{r} 2 \\ +0 \\ \hline \end{array}$$

$$\begin{array}{r} 8 \\ +1 \\ \hline \end{array}$$

$$\begin{array}{r} 8 \\ +0 \\ \hline \end{array}$$

$$\begin{array}{r} 2 \\ +5 \\ \hline \end{array}$$

$$\begin{array}{r} 4 \\ +2 \\ \hline \end{array}$$

$$\begin{array}{r} 3 \\ +7 \\ \hline \end{array}$$

$$\begin{array}{r} 7 \\ +2 \\ \hline \end{array}$$

$$\begin{array}{r} 6 \\ +1 \\ \hline \end{array}$$

$$\begin{array}{r} 4 \\ +3 \\ \hline \end{array}$$

$$\begin{array}{r} 1 \\ +0 \\ \hline \end{array}$$

$$\begin{array}{r} 0 \\ +5 \\ \hline \end{array}$$

$$\begin{array}{r} 4 \\ +4 \\ \hline \end{array}$$

$$\begin{array}{r} 0 \\ +0 \\ \hline \end{array}$$

$$\begin{array}{r} 9 \\ +4 \\ \hline \end{array}$$

$$\begin{array}{r} 3 \\ +5 \\ \hline \end{array}$$

$$\begin{array}{r} 5 \\ +1 \\ \hline \end{array}$$

$$\begin{array}{r} 6 \\ +9 \\ \hline \end{array}$$

$$\begin{array}{r} 4 \\ +5 \\ \hline \end{array}$$

Lose one turn.

FS-23241 One-Minute Math Level A Addition

Move ahead one.

$$7+0$$

$$9+2$$

$$1+1$$

$$5+4$$

$$4+0$$

$$3+1$$

$$9+6$$

$$9+0$$

$$6+0$$

$$2+2$$

$$4+3$$

$$0+0$$

$$9+1$$

$$2+1$$

$$2+3$$

$$5+3$$

$$1+1$$

$$8+2$$

$$0+3$$

$$4+1$$

FS-23241 One-Minute Math Level A Addition

Awards

Awards

I Know My Addition Facts 0 to 10!

I Climbed the Math Fact Tree!

Award: Official Fact Finder

FS-23241 One-Minute Math Level A Addition

Certificates

Congratulations!

_____

has completed Level A Addition
Sums 0 to 10

Great Work!

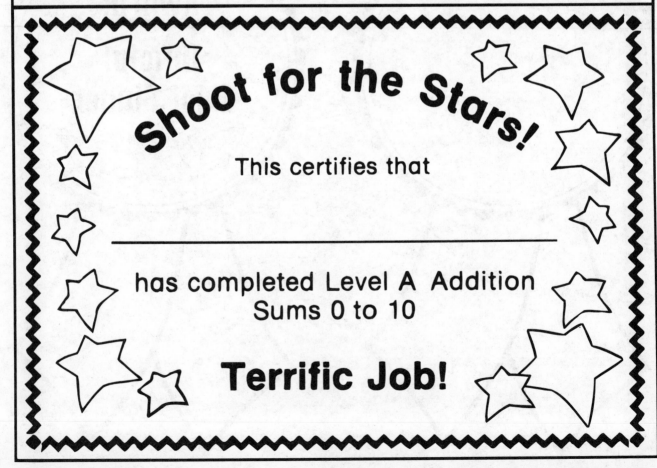

Shoot for the Stars!

This certifies that

_____

has completed Level A Addition
Sums 0 to 10

Terrific Job!

Certificates

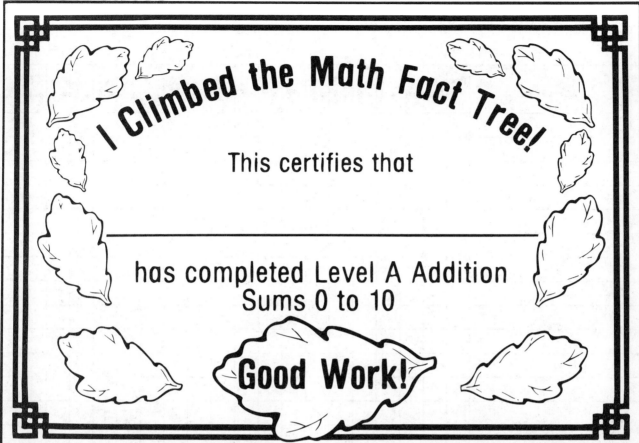

I Climbed the Math Fact Tree!

This certifies that

_____

has completed Level A Addition
Sums 0 to 10

Good Work!

Congratulations!

_____

has completed Level A Addition
Sums 0 to 10

Great Job!

Progress Chart
Level A Addition   Sums 0 to 10

Name	Pre-test	0 Rule	1 Rule	2 + 2	2 + 3	2 + 4	2 + 5	2 + 6	2 + 7	2 + 8	3 + 3	3 + 4	3 + 5	3 + 6	3 + 7	4 + 4	4 + 5	4 + 6	5 + 5	Test

FS-23241 One-Minute Math Level A Addition

Student Progress Chart

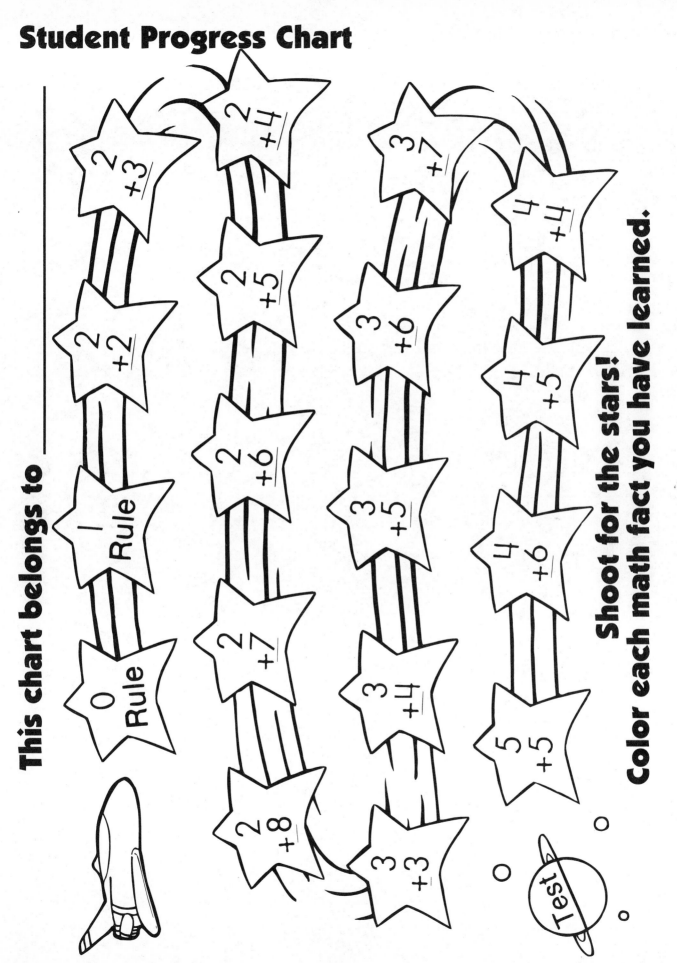

This chart belongs to

Shoot for the stars!
Color each math fact you have learned.

FS-23241 One-Minute Math Level A Addition

2	5	8	5	4
+ 6	+ 4	+ 2	+ 3	+ 3

3	0	4	1	6
+ 3	+ 4	+ 5	+ 6	+ 4

3	1	2	2	2
+ 5	+ 9	+ 2	+ 3	+ 7

4	2	3	5	7
+ 6	+ 4	+ 6	+ 2	+ 3

7	4	3	9	5
+ 2	+ 4	+ 4	+ 0	+ 5

6	3	2	6	2
+ 2	+ 7	+ 8	+ 3	+ 5

1

Name _____

4 + 0	0 + 0	10 + 0	0 + 1	0 + 6
0 + 8	0 + 10	0 + 5	0 + 2	7 + 0
0 + 9	1 + 0	9 + 0	0 + 3	0 + 8
0 + 6	3 + 0	0 + 2	0 + 9	0 + 7
0 + 4	6 + 0	9 + 0	0 + 0	0 + 1
2 + 0	10 + 0	0 + 8	5 + 0	0 + 4

Name _____

9 + 0	0 + 1	0 + 4	0 + 0	6 + 0
7 + 0	0 + 10	0 + 8	0 + 2	0 + 5
2 + 0	0 + 8	5 + 0	10 + 0	0 + 4
0 + 1	10 + 0	4 + 0	0 + 1	0 + 0
9 + 0	0 + 3	1 + 0	0 + 9	0 + 8
3 + 0	0 + 7	0 + 6	0 + 9	0 + 2

Name _____

$$\begin{array}{r} 1 \\ + 4 \\ \hline \end{array} \qquad \begin{array}{r} 3 \\ + 0 \\ \hline \end{array} \qquad \begin{array}{r} 5 \\ + 1 \\ \hline \end{array} \qquad \begin{array}{r} 1 \\ + 8 \\ \hline \end{array} \qquad \begin{array}{r} 0 \\ + 4 \\ \hline \end{array}$$

$$\begin{array}{r} 6 \\ + 0 \\ \hline \end{array} \qquad \begin{array}{r} 0 \\ + 0 \\ \hline \end{array} \qquad \begin{array}{r} 0 \\ + 7 \\ \hline \end{array} \qquad \begin{array}{r} 3 \\ + 1 \\ \hline \end{array} \qquad \begin{array}{r} 1 \\ + 6 \\ \hline \end{array}$$

$$\begin{array}{r} 1 \\ + 1 \\ \hline \end{array} \qquad \begin{array}{r} 1 \\ + 9 \\ \hline \end{array} \qquad \begin{array}{r} 7 \\ + 1 \\ \hline \end{array} \qquad \begin{array}{r} 9 \\ + 0 \\ \hline \end{array} \qquad \begin{array}{r} 1 \\ + 2 \\ \hline \end{array}$$

$$\begin{array}{r} 1 \\ + 7 \\ \hline \end{array} \qquad \begin{array}{r} 1 \\ + 0 \\ \hline \end{array} \qquad \begin{array}{r} 0 \\ + 10 \\ \hline \end{array} \qquad \begin{array}{r} 7 \\ + 0 \\ \hline \end{array} \qquad \begin{array}{r} 1 \\ + 8 \\ \hline \end{array}$$

$$\begin{array}{r} 1 \\ + 5 \\ \hline \end{array} \qquad \begin{array}{r} 1 \\ + 3 \\ \hline \end{array} \qquad \begin{array}{r} 5 \\ + 0 \\ \hline \end{array} \qquad \begin{array}{r} 6 \\ + 1 \\ \hline \end{array} \qquad \begin{array}{r} 0 \\ + 9 \\ \hline \end{array}$$

$$\begin{array}{r} 4 \\ + 1 \\ \hline \end{array} \qquad \begin{array}{r} 0 \\ + 6 \\ \hline \end{array} \qquad \begin{array}{r} 9 \\ + 1 \\ \hline \end{array} \qquad \begin{array}{r} 8 \\ + 0 \\ \hline \end{array} \qquad \begin{array}{r} 0 \\ + 2 \\ \hline \end{array}$$

Name _____

0 + 2	9 + 1	0 + 6	4 + 1	8 + 0
1 + 2	9 + 0	1 + 1	7 + 1	1 + 9
0 + 4	1 + 4	5 + 1	3 + 0	1 + 8
1 + 5	6 + 1	5 + 0	1 + 3	0 + 9
1 + 8	1 + 7	7 + 0	0 + 10	1 + 0
3 + 1	0 + 7	1 + 6	0 + 0	3 + 1

Name _____

0 + 1	2 + 2	1 + 3	2 + 2	6 + 1
2 + 2	9 + 0	2 + 2	0 + 2	1 + 7
2 + 2	1 + 2	2 + 2	3 + 0	2 + 2
1 + 1	2 + 2	8 + 1	7 + 1	1 + 4
2 + 2	0 + 4	9 + 1	2 + 2	5 + 1
8 + 0	2 + 2	0 + 5	1 + 6	2 + 2

Level A 2+2
Practice Page B

Name _____

```
   2        8        1        2        0
 + 2      + 0      + 6      + 2      + 5
 ___      ___      ___      ___      ___


   1        2        7        8        2
 + 1      + 2      + 1      + 1      + 2
 ___      ___      ___      ___      ___


   0        1        2        6        2
 + 1      + 3      + 2      + 1      + 2
 ___      ___      ___      ___      ___


   2        0        5        2        9
 + 2      + 4      + 1      + 2      + 1
 ___      ___      ___      ___      ___


   9        2        0        1        2
 + 0      + 2      + 2      + 7      + 2
 ___      ___      ___      ___      ___


   2        1        2        3        1
 + 2      + 4      + 2      + 0      + 2
 ___      ___      ___      ___      ___
```

FS-23241 One-Minute Math Level A Addition

Name _____

8 + 0	3 + 2	5 + 1	2 + 2	3 + 2
1 + 8	0 + 6	2 + 3	0 + 4	2 + 3
3 + 2	1 + 3	2 + 2	2 + 3	2 + 0
9 + 1	3 + 2	0 + 7	2 + 2	2 + 3
2 + 3	9 + 0	2 + 2	3 + 2	1 + 1
2 + 2	2 + 3	1 + 4	2 + 2	2 + 3

Name _____

0 + 4	2 + 3	1 + 8	2 + 3	0 + 6
3 + 2	0 + 7	9 + 1	2 + 2	2 + 3
1 + 4	2 + 3	2 + 2	3 + 2	2 + 2
2 + 2	5 + 1	3 + 2	8 + 0	3 + 2
2 + 3	2 + 2	1 + 3	3 + 2	2 + 0
1 + 1	2 + 2	2 + 3	9 + 0	3 + 2

Name _____

$$
\begin{array}{r} 2 \\ + 2 \\ \hline \end{array}
\qquad
\begin{array}{r} 4 \\ + 2 \\ \hline \end{array}
\qquad
\begin{array}{r} 3 \\ + 0 \\ \hline \end{array}
\qquad
\begin{array}{r} 2 \\ + 4 \\ \hline \end{array}
\qquad
\begin{array}{r} 1 \\ + 1 \\ \hline \end{array}
$$

$$
\begin{array}{r} 2 \\ + 4 \\ \hline \end{array}
\qquad
\begin{array}{r} 2 \\ + 3 \\ \hline \end{array}
\qquad
\begin{array}{r} 3 \\ + 1 \\ \hline \end{array}
\qquad
\begin{array}{r} 6 \\ + 0 \\ \hline \end{array}
\qquad
\begin{array}{r} 4 \\ + 2 \\ \hline \end{array}
$$

$$
\begin{array}{r} 2 \\ + 2 \\ \hline \end{array}
\qquad
\begin{array}{r} 4 \\ + 2 \\ \hline \end{array}
\qquad
\begin{array}{r} 5 \\ + 1 \\ \hline \end{array}
\qquad
\begin{array}{r} 2 \\ + 3 \\ \hline \end{array}
\qquad
\begin{array}{r} 2 \\ + 4 \\ \hline \end{array}
$$

$$
\begin{array}{r} 4 \\ + 2 \\ \hline \end{array}
\qquad
\begin{array}{r} 9 \\ + 0 \\ \hline \end{array}
\qquad
\begin{array}{r} 2 \\ + 4 \\ \hline \end{array}
\qquad
\begin{array}{r} 1 \\ + 8 \\ \hline \end{array}
\qquad
\begin{array}{r} 3 \\ + 2 \\ \hline \end{array}
$$

$$
\begin{array}{r} 1 \\ + 0 \\ \hline \end{array}
\qquad
\begin{array}{r} 2 \\ + 4 \\ \hline \end{array}
\qquad
\begin{array}{r} 2 \\ + 3 \\ \hline \end{array}
\qquad
\begin{array}{r} 4 \\ + 2 \\ \hline \end{array}
\qquad
\begin{array}{r} 2 \\ + 2 \\ \hline \end{array}
$$

$$
\begin{array}{r} 2 \\ + 4 \\ \hline \end{array}
\qquad
\begin{array}{r} 3 \\ + 2 \\ \hline \end{array}
\qquad
\begin{array}{r} 0 \\ + 4 \\ \hline \end{array}
\qquad
\begin{array}{r} 1 \\ + 2 \\ \hline \end{array}
\qquad
\begin{array}{r} 2 \\ + 4 \\ \hline \end{array}
$$

Name _____

```
   2        3        4        6        2
+  4     +  1     +  2     +  0     +  3
____     ____     ____     ____     ____


   5        4        2        2        3
+  1     +  2     +  2     +  4     +  2
____     ____     ____     ____     ____


   2        2        2        1        4
+  4     +  2     +  3     +  0     +  2
____     ____     ____     ____     ____


   2        4        3        1        2
+  2     +  2     +  0     +  1     +  4
____     ____     ____     ____     ____


   2        0        1        2        3
+  4     +  4     +  2     +  4     +  2
____     ____     ____     ____     ____


   1        3        4        9        2
+  8     +  2     +  2     +  0     +  4
____     ____     ____     ____     ____
```

Level A 2+5
Practice Page A

$$
\begin{array}{r} 5 \\ + 2 \\ \hline \end{array}
\qquad
\begin{array}{r} 0 \\ + 8 \\ \hline \end{array}
\qquad
\begin{array}{r} 4 \\ + 2 \\ \hline \end{array}
\qquad
\begin{array}{r} 2 \\ + 5 \\ \hline \end{array}
\qquad
\begin{array}{r} 2 \\ + 3 \\ \hline \end{array}
$$

$$
\begin{array}{r} 2 \\ + 4 \\ \hline \end{array}
\qquad
\begin{array}{r} 5 \\ + 2 \\ \hline \end{array}
\qquad
\begin{array}{r} 9 \\ + 1 \\ \hline \end{array}
\qquad
\begin{array}{r} 2 \\ + 2 \\ \hline \end{array}
\qquad
\begin{array}{r} 5 \\ + 2 \\ \hline \end{array}
$$

$$
\begin{array}{r} 2 \\ + 5 \\ \hline \end{array}
\qquad
\begin{array}{r} 3 \\ + 2 \\ \hline \end{array}
\qquad
\begin{array}{r} 5 \\ + 0 \\ \hline \end{array}
\qquad
\begin{array}{r} 2 \\ + 5 \\ \hline \end{array}
\qquad
\begin{array}{r} 2 \\ + 4 \\ \hline \end{array}
$$

$$
\begin{array}{r} 4 \\ + 2 \\ \hline \end{array}
\qquad
\begin{array}{r} 5 \\ + 2 \\ \hline \end{array}
\qquad
\begin{array}{r} 1 \\ + 7 \\ \hline \end{array}
\qquad
\begin{array}{r} 2 \\ + 3 \\ \hline \end{array}
\qquad
\begin{array}{r} 2 \\ + 5 \\ \hline \end{array}
$$

$$
\begin{array}{r} 2 \\ + 5 \\ \hline \end{array}
\qquad
\begin{array}{r} 2 \\ + 2 \\ \hline \end{array}
\qquad
\begin{array}{r} 2 \\ + 4 \\ \hline \end{array}
\qquad
\begin{array}{r} 5 \\ + 2 \\ \hline \end{array}
\qquad
\begin{array}{r} 0 \\ + 0 \\ \hline \end{array}
$$

$$
\begin{array}{r} 1 \\ + 6 \\ \hline \end{array}
\qquad
\begin{array}{r} 2 \\ + 5 \\ \hline \end{array}
\qquad
\begin{array}{r} 2 \\ + 2 \\ \hline \end{array}
\qquad
\begin{array}{r} 4 \\ + 2 \\ \hline \end{array}
\qquad
\begin{array}{r} 5 \\ + 2 \\ \hline \end{array}
$$

Level A 2+5
Practice Page B

$$
\begin{array}{r} 3 \\ + 2 \\ \hline \end{array}
\qquad
\begin{array}{r} 5 \\ + 0 \\ \hline \end{array}
\qquad
\begin{array}{r} 2 \\ + 5 \\ \hline \end{array}
\qquad
\begin{array}{r} 2 \\ + 4 \\ \hline \end{array}
\qquad
\begin{array}{r} 5 \\ + 2 \\ \hline \end{array}
$$

$$
\begin{array}{r} 2 \\ + 5 \\ \hline \end{array}
\qquad
\begin{array}{r} 0 \\ + 0 \\ \hline \end{array}
\qquad
\begin{array}{r} 2 \\ + 2 \\ \hline \end{array}
\qquad
\begin{array}{r} 5 \\ + 2 \\ \hline \end{array}
\qquad
\begin{array}{r} 2 \\ + 4 \\ \hline \end{array}
$$

$$
\begin{array}{r} 0 \\ + 8 \\ \hline \end{array}
\qquad
\begin{array}{r} 5 \\ + 2 \\ \hline \end{array}
\qquad
\begin{array}{r} 2 \\ + 3 \\ \hline \end{array}
\qquad
\begin{array}{r} 2 \\ + 5 \\ \hline \end{array}
\qquad
\begin{array}{r} 4 \\ + 2 \\ \hline \end{array}
$$

$$
\begin{array}{r} 5 \\ + 2 \\ \hline \end{array}
\qquad
\begin{array}{r} 1 \\ + 6 \\ \hline \end{array}
\qquad
\begin{array}{r} 2 \\ + 5 \\ \hline \end{array}
\qquad
\begin{array}{r} 4 \\ + 2 \\ \hline \end{array}
\qquad
\begin{array}{r} 2 \\ + 2 \\ \hline \end{array}
$$

$$
\begin{array}{r} 9 \\ + 1 \\ \hline \end{array}
\qquad
\begin{array}{r} 2 \\ + 5 \\ \hline \end{array}
\qquad
\begin{array}{r} 2 \\ + 2 \\ \hline \end{array}
\qquad
\begin{array}{r} 2 \\ + 4 \\ \hline \end{array}
\qquad
\begin{array}{r} 5 \\ + 2 \\ \hline \end{array}
$$

$$
\begin{array}{r} 2 \\ + 5 \\ \hline \end{array}
\qquad
\begin{array}{r} 1 \\ + 7 \\ \hline \end{array}
\qquad
\begin{array}{r} 4 \\ + 2 \\ \hline \end{array}
\qquad
\begin{array}{r} 5 \\ + 2 \\ \hline \end{array}
\qquad
\begin{array}{r} 2 \\ + 3 \\ \hline \end{array}
$$

Name _____

4	2	5	6	2
+ 2	+ 6	+ 2	+ 2	+ 3

6	2	4	2	2
+ 2	+ 1	+ 2	+ 5	+ 6

2	2	1	2	2
+ 3	+ 6	+ 0	+ 6	+ 4

6	2	2	2	5
+ 2	+ 2	+ 6	+ 3	+ 2

2	2	2	4	6
+ 4	+ 6	+ 5	+ 0	+ 2

6	9	6	2	2
+ 2	+ 0	+ 2	+ 4	+ 5

Name _____

6 + 2	5 + 2	2 + 6	2 + 2	2 + 3
2 + 3	2 + 6	5 + 2	6 + 2	4 + 2
2 + 5	2 + 4	6 + 2	9 + 0	6 + 2
2 + 6	1 + 0	2 + 3	2 + 6	1 + 0
2 + 5	6 + 2	4 + 2	2 + 1	2 + 6
6 + 2	4 + 0	2 + 5	2 + 6	2 + 4

Name _____

0	2	2	1	7
+ 9	+ 7	+ 5	+ 8	+ 2

7	5	2	2	6
+ 2	+ 2	+ 7	+ 4	+ 2

2	2	2	7	3
+ 6	+ 7	+ 5	+ 2	+ 2

4	1	2	6	7
+ 0	+ 4	+ 7	+ 2	+ 2

2	2	4	7	2
+ 7	+ 6	+ 2	+ 2	+ 2

2	7	3	6	2
+ 3	+ 2	+ 1	+ 2	+ 7

Name _____

7 + 2	2 + 6	4 + 2	2 + 2	2 + 7
1 + 8	2 + 7	0 + 9	7 + 2	2 + 5
7 + 2	3 + 1	2 + 7	2 + 3	6 + 2
4 + 0	2 + 7	6 + 2	1 + 4	7 + 2
6 + 2	7 + 2	5 + 2	2 + 7	2 + 4
3 + 2	2 + 5	7 + 2	2 + 6	2 + 7

Level A 2+8
Practice Page A

Name _____

0 + 9	8 + 2	2 + 7	6 + 0	2 + 8
6 + 1	2 + 4	8 + 2	1 + 7	7 + 2
2 + 8	2 + 7	2 + 8	5 + 2	8 + 2
1 + 8	8 + 2	1 + 5	2 + 8	7 + 2
8 + 2	4 + 1	2 + 8	2 + 3	8 + 2
9 + 1	2 + 8	2 + 2	7 + 2	2 + 6

Name _____

$$\begin{array}{r} 9 \\ +\ 1 \\ \hline \end{array} \qquad \begin{array}{r} 2 \\ +\ 6 \\ \hline \end{array} \qquad \begin{array}{r} 2 \\ +\ 8 \\ \hline \end{array} \qquad \begin{array}{r} 2 \\ +\ 2 \\ \hline \end{array} \qquad \begin{array}{r} 7 \\ +\ 2 \\ \hline \end{array}$$

$$\begin{array}{r} 8 \\ +\ 2 \\ \hline \end{array} \qquad \begin{array}{r} 5 \\ +\ 2 \\ \hline \end{array} \qquad \begin{array}{r} 2 \\ +\ 8 \\ \hline \end{array} \qquad \begin{array}{r} 2 \\ +\ 7 \\ \hline \end{array} \qquad \begin{array}{r} 2 \\ +\ 8 \\ \hline \end{array}$$

$$\begin{array}{r} 6 \\ +\ 0 \\ \hline \end{array} \qquad \begin{array}{r} 8 \\ +\ 2 \\ \hline \end{array} \qquad \begin{array}{r} 0 \\ +\ 9 \\ \hline \end{array} \qquad \begin{array}{r} 2 \\ +\ 8 \\ \hline \end{array} \qquad \begin{array}{r} 2 \\ +\ 7 \\ \hline \end{array}$$

$$\begin{array}{r} 2 \\ +\ 8 \\ \hline \end{array} \qquad \begin{array}{r} 2 \\ +\ 3 \\ \hline \end{array} \qquad \begin{array}{r} 8 \\ +\ 2 \\ \hline \end{array} \qquad \begin{array}{r} 4 \\ +\ 1 \\ \hline \end{array} \qquad \begin{array}{r} 2 \\ +\ 8 \\ \hline \end{array}$$

$$\begin{array}{r} 1 \\ +\ 7 \\ \hline \end{array} \qquad \begin{array}{r} 7 \\ +\ 2 \\ \hline \end{array} \qquad \begin{array}{r} 2 \\ +\ 4 \\ \hline \end{array} \qquad \begin{array}{r} 8 \\ +\ 2 \\ \hline \end{array} \qquad \begin{array}{r} 6 \\ +\ 1 \\ \hline \end{array}$$

$$\begin{array}{r} 2 \\ +\ 8 \\ \hline \end{array} \qquad \begin{array}{r} 1 \\ +\ 5 \\ \hline \end{array} \qquad \begin{array}{r} 7 \\ +\ 2 \\ \hline \end{array} \qquad \begin{array}{r} 1 \\ +\ 8 \\ \hline \end{array} \qquad \begin{array}{r} 8 \\ +\ 2 \\ \hline \end{array}$$

Name _____

2 + 6	3 + 3	5 + 2	3 + 3	2 + 8
3 + 3	3 + 2	1 + 8	2 + 7	3 + 3
0 + 6	8 + 2	3 + 3	2 + 2	3 + 3
4 + 2	3 + 3	2 + 6	3 + 3	2 + 8
3 + 3	2 + 8	3 + 3	8 + 2	2 + 7
8 + 2	3 + 3	7 + 2	2 + 5	3 + 3

Name _____

3 + 3	5 + 2	3 + 3	2 + 6	2 + 8
7 + 2	2 + 5	3 + 3	8 + 2	3 + 3
2 + 2	3 + 3	8 + 2	3 + 3	0 + 6
3 + 3	2 + 8	3 + 3	4 + 2	2 + 6
1 + 8	3 + 3	2 + 7	3 + 2	3 + 3
3 + 3	2 + 8	2 + 7	3 + 3	8 + 2

Name _____

$$
\begin{array}{r} 8 \\ +\ 2 \\ \hline \end{array}
\qquad
\begin{array}{r} 4 \\ +\ 3 \\ \hline \end{array}
\qquad
\begin{array}{r} 3 \\ +\ 3 \\ \hline \end{array}
\qquad
\begin{array}{r} 2 \\ +\ 3 \\ \hline \end{array}
\qquad
\begin{array}{r} 3 \\ +\ 4 \\ \hline \end{array}
$$

$$
\begin{array}{r} 3 \\ +\ 4 \\ \hline \end{array}
\qquad
\begin{array}{r} 2 \\ +\ 4 \\ \hline \end{array}
\qquad
\begin{array}{r} 6 \\ +\ 2 \\ \hline \end{array}
\qquad
\begin{array}{r} 4 \\ +\ 3 \\ \hline \end{array}
\qquad
\begin{array}{r} 3 \\ +\ 3 \\ \hline \end{array}
$$

$$
\begin{array}{r} 7 \\ +\ 2 \\ \hline \end{array}
\qquad
\begin{array}{r} 2 \\ +\ 8 \\ \hline \end{array}
\qquad
\begin{array}{r} 4 \\ +\ 3 \\ \hline \end{array}
\qquad
\begin{array}{r} 5 \\ +\ 2 \\ \hline \end{array}
\qquad
\begin{array}{r} 3 \\ +\ 4 \\ \hline \end{array}
$$

$$
\begin{array}{r} 3 \\ +\ 3 \\ \hline \end{array}
\qquad
\begin{array}{r} 3 \\ +\ 4 \\ \hline \end{array}
\qquad
\begin{array}{r} 1 \\ +\ 6 \\ \hline \end{array}
\qquad
\begin{array}{r} 4 \\ +\ 3 \\ \hline \end{array}
\qquad
\begin{array}{r} 0 \\ +\ 9 \\ \hline \end{array}
$$

$$
\begin{array}{r} 4 \\ +\ 3 \\ \hline \end{array}
\qquad
\begin{array}{r} 2 \\ +\ 2 \\ \hline \end{array}
\qquad
\begin{array}{r} 3 \\ +\ 4 \\ \hline \end{array}
\qquad
\begin{array}{r} 3 \\ +\ 3 \\ \hline \end{array}
\qquad
\begin{array}{r} 6 \\ +\ 2 \\ \hline \end{array}
$$

$$
\begin{array}{r} 3 \\ +\ 3 \\ \hline \end{array}
\qquad
\begin{array}{r} 4 \\ +\ 3 \\ \hline \end{array}
\qquad
\begin{array}{r} 2 \\ +\ 7 \\ \hline \end{array}
\qquad
\begin{array}{r} 4 \\ +\ 2 \\ \hline \end{array}
\qquad
\begin{array}{r} 3 \\ +\ 4 \\ \hline \end{array}
$$

FS-23241 One-Minute Math Level A Addition

Name _____

4 + 3	6 + 2	2 + 4	3 + 3	3 + 4
2 + 3	3 + 3	3 + 4	8 + 2	4 + 3
3 + 4	2 + 7	3 + 3	4 + 3	4 + 2
2 + 8	4 + 3	5 + 2	7 + 2	3 + 4
4 + 3	6 + 2	2 + 2	3 + 4	3 + 3
1 + 6	3 + 4	3 + 3	4 + 3	0 + 9

5 + 3	2 + 6	8 + 2	3 + 5	4 + 3
3 + 2	5 + 3	1 + 6	3 + 4	3 + 5
3 + 5	2 + 2	0 + 9	5 + 3	2 + 7
3 + 3	5 + 3	4 + 3	5 + 2	3 + 5
3 + 5	2 + 4	5 + 3	2 + 8	3 + 4
3 + 3	5 + 3	3 + 4	3 + 5	2 + 3

Name _____

0 + 9	5 + 3	2 + 2	3 + 5	2 + 7
3 + 5	1 + 6	5 + 3	3 + 4	3 + 2
2 + 3	3 + 4	3 + 5	3 + 3	5 + 3
3 + 5	8 + 2	4 + 3	5 + 3	2 + 6
4 + 3	5 + 3	3 + 3	5 + 2	3 + 5
2 + 8	3 + 5	2 + 4	5 + 3	3 + 4

Name _____

2 + 4	3 + 6	4 + 3	5 + 2	6 + 3
3 + 6	1 + 3	6 + 3	2 + 6	3 + 5
5 + 3	6 + 3	3 + 2	3 + 6	8 + 2
6 + 3	2 + 7	3 + 5	3 + 4	3 + 6
2 + 2	6 + 3	3 + 6	0 + 3	5 + 3
3 + 6	3 + 5	8 + 2	6 + 3	3 + 3

Level A 3+6
Practice Page B

Name _____

3 + 5	2 + 7	6 + 3	3 + 4	6 + 3
3 + 3	3 + 6	8 + 2	6 + 3	3 + 5
3 + 6	4 + 3	6 + 3	5 + 2	2 + 4
6 + 3	0 + 3	2 + 2	5 + 3	3 + 6
1 + 3	3 + 6	2 + 6	3 + 5	6 + 3
3 + 6	3 + 2	8 + 2	6 + 3	5 + 3

FS-23241 One-Minute Math Level A Addition

Name _____

3 + 6	2 + 2	3 + 7	2 + 4	7 + 3
7 + 3	3 + 2	3 + 5	3 + 7	6 + 2
2 + 8	7 + 3	3 + 4	3 + 6	3 + 7
3 + 7	6 + 3	7 + 2	7 + 3	3 + 3
2 + 5	3 + 7	1 + 8	3 + 6	7 + 3
7 + 3	3 + 4	3 + 7	0 + 6	6 + 3

Name _____

1 + 8	3 + 7	2 + 5	7 + 3	3 + 6
3 + 7	2 + 2	3 + 6	2 + 4	7 + 3
0 + 6	3 + 4	7 + 3	6 + 3	3 + 7
3 + 2	7 + 3	3 + 5	3 + 7	6 + 2
3 + 7	3 + 3	6 + 3	7 + 3	7 + 2
2 + 8	7 + 3	3 + 4	3 + 6	3 + 7

FS-23241 One-Minute Math Level A Addition

Name _____

4 + 4	3 + 5	4 + 4	3 + 7	4 + 2
0 + 5	4 + 4	2 + 6	2 + 2	4 + 4
4 + 4	8 + 2	4 + 4	6 + 3	3 + 7
3 + 2	2 + 5	4 + 4	7 + 3	4 + 4
4 + 4	3 + 4	3 + 3	4 + 4	7 + 3
1 + 6	4 + 4	3 + 7	4 + 4	7 + 2

Name _____

$$
\begin{array}{r} 5 \\ + 4 \\ \hline \end{array}
\qquad
\begin{array}{r} 2 \\ + 8 \\ \hline \end{array}
\qquad
\begin{array}{r} 3 \\ + 7 \\ \hline \end{array}
\qquad
\begin{array}{r} 4 \\ + 5 \\ \hline \end{array}
\qquad
\begin{array}{r} 4 \\ + 2 \\ \hline \end{array}
$$

$$
\begin{array}{r} 3 \\ + 4 \\ \hline \end{array}
\qquad
\begin{array}{r} 4 \\ + 5 \\ \hline \end{array}
\qquad
\begin{array}{r} 4 \\ + 4 \\ \hline \end{array}
\qquad
\begin{array}{r} 3 \\ + 3 \\ \hline \end{array}
\qquad
\begin{array}{r} 5 \\ + 4 \\ \hline \end{array}
$$

$$
\begin{array}{r} 4 \\ + 5 \\ \hline \end{array}
\qquad
\begin{array}{r} 3 \\ + 6 \\ \hline \end{array}
\qquad
\begin{array}{r} 5 \\ + 4 \\ \hline \end{array}
\qquad
\begin{array}{r} 3 \\ + 2 \\ \hline \end{array}
\qquad
\begin{array}{r} 4 \\ + 4 \\ \hline \end{array}
$$

$$
\begin{array}{r} 4 \\ + 4 \\ \hline \end{array}
\qquad
\begin{array}{r} 5 \\ + 4 \\ \hline \end{array}
\qquad
\begin{array}{r} 7 \\ + 2 \\ \hline \end{array}
\qquad
\begin{array}{r} 4 \\ + 5 \\ \hline \end{array}
\qquad
\begin{array}{r} 3 \\ + 4 \\ \hline \end{array}
$$

$$
\begin{array}{r} 4 \\ + 5 \\ \hline \end{array}
\qquad
\begin{array}{r} 6 \\ + 2 \\ \hline \end{array}
\qquad
\begin{array}{r} 4 \\ + 4 \\ \hline \end{array}
\qquad
\begin{array}{r} 2 \\ + 5 \\ \hline \end{array}
\qquad
\begin{array}{r} 5 \\ + 4 \\ \hline \end{array}
$$

$$
\begin{array}{r} 3 \\ + 5 \\ \hline \end{array}
\qquad
\begin{array}{r} 5 \\ + 4 \\ \hline \end{array}
\qquad
\begin{array}{r} 3 \\ + 4 \\ \hline \end{array}
\qquad
\begin{array}{r} 4 \\ + 5 \\ \hline \end{array}
\qquad
\begin{array}{r} 4 \\ + 4 \\ \hline \end{array}
$$

© Frank Schaffer Publications, Inc. 32 FS-23241 One-Minute Math Level A Addition

Name _____

5 + 4	2 + 8	3 + 7	4 + 5	4 + 2
3 + 4	4 + 5	4 + 4	3 + 3	5 + 4
4 + 5	3 + 6	5 + 4	3 + 2	4 + 4
4 + 4	5 + 4	7 + 2	4 + 5	3 + 4
4 + 5	6 + 2	4 + 4	2 + 5	5 + 4
3 + 5	5 + 4	3 + 4	4 + 5	4 + 4

2 + 8	5 + 4	4 + 6	4 + 5	3 + 7
5 + 4	3 + 4	3 + 5	4 + 4	4 + 5
7 + 2	4 + 4	5 + 4	3 + 4	4 + 5
5 + 4	3 + 3	4 + 4	4 + 5	3 + 4
6 + 2	4 + 5	2 + 5	4 + 4	5 + 4
4 + 5	3 + 6	5 + 4	3 + 2	4 + 4

Level A 4+6
Practice Page A

$$\begin{array}{r} 6 \\ +\ 4 \\ \hline \end{array} \qquad \begin{array}{r} 4 \\ +\ 5 \\ \hline \end{array} \qquad \begin{array}{r} 3 \\ +\ 7 \\ \hline \end{array} \qquad \begin{array}{r} 4 \\ +\ 6 \\ \hline \end{array} \qquad \begin{array}{r} 6 \\ +\ 2 \\ \hline \end{array}$$

$$\begin{array}{r} 1 \\ +\ 7 \\ \hline \end{array} \qquad \begin{array}{r} 4 \\ +\ 6 \\ \hline \end{array} \qquad \begin{array}{r} 2 \\ +\ 5 \\ \hline \end{array} \qquad \begin{array}{r} 8 \\ +\ 2 \\ \hline \end{array} \qquad \begin{array}{r} 6 \\ +\ 4 \\ \hline \end{array}$$

$$\begin{array}{r} 6 \\ +\ 4 \\ \hline \end{array} \qquad \begin{array}{r} 3 \\ +\ 3 \\ \hline \end{array} \qquad \begin{array}{r} 5 \\ +\ 4 \\ \hline \end{array} \qquad \begin{array}{r} 4 \\ +\ 6 \\ \hline \end{array} \qquad \begin{array}{r} 6 \\ +\ 3 \\ \hline \end{array}$$

$$\begin{array}{r} 4 \\ +\ 5 \\ \hline \end{array} \qquad \begin{array}{r} 4 \\ +\ 6 \\ \hline \end{array} \qquad \begin{array}{r} 2 \\ +\ 4 \\ \hline \end{array} \qquad \begin{array}{r} 7 \\ +\ 2 \\ \hline \end{array} \qquad \begin{array}{r} 6 \\ +\ 4 \\ \hline \end{array}$$

$$\begin{array}{r} 4 \\ +\ 3 \\ \hline \end{array} \qquad \begin{array}{r} 5 \\ +\ 4 \\ \hline \end{array} \qquad \begin{array}{r} 6 \\ +\ 4 \\ \hline \end{array} \qquad \begin{array}{r} 3 \\ +\ 2 \\ \hline \end{array} \qquad \begin{array}{r} 4 \\ +\ 6 \\ \hline \end{array}$$

$$\begin{array}{r} 4 \\ +\ 6 \\ \hline \end{array} \qquad \begin{array}{r} 4 \\ +\ 4 \\ \hline \end{array} \qquad \begin{array}{r} 4 \\ +\ 5 \\ \hline \end{array} \qquad \begin{array}{r} 6 \\ +\ 4 \\ \hline \end{array} \qquad \begin{array}{r} 3 \\ +\ 5 \\ \hline \end{array}$$

Level A 4+6
Practice Page B

Name _____

$$6 + 4 \qquad 8 + 2 \qquad 2 + 5 \qquad 1 + 7 \qquad 4 + 6$$

$$4 + 5 \qquad 3 + 7 \qquad 4 + 6 \qquad 2 + 6 \qquad 6 + 4$$

$$4 + 4 \qquad 6 + 4 \qquad 4 + 5 \qquad 4 + 6 \qquad 3 + 5$$

$$3 + 3 \qquad 6 + 3 \qquad 4 + 6 \qquad 5 + 4 \qquad 6 + 4$$

$$4 + 6 \qquad 3 + 2 \qquad 6 + 4 \qquad 5 + 4 \qquad 4 + 3$$

$$2 + 4 \qquad 6 + 4 \qquad 7 + 2 \qquad 4 + 5 \qquad 4 + 6$$

Level A 5+5
Practice Page A

Name _____

6 + 2	5 + 5	3 + 7	5 + 5	5 + 2
5 + 5	6 + 3	4 + 6	2 + 4	5 + 5
5 + 5	2 + 8	5 + 5	4 + 5	6 + 4
4 + 6	5 + 5	2 + 3	5 + 5	3 + 3
4 + 4	5 + 3	5 + 5	6 + 4	5 + 5
5 + 5	6 + 4	4 + 3	5 + 5	2 + 7

Name _____

6 + 4	2 + 8	5 + 5	4 + 5	5 + 5
2 + 7	5 + 5	6 + 4	5 + 5	4 + 3
5 + 5	3 + 7	5 + 2	5 + 5	6 + 2
4 + 4	5 + 5	6 + 4	5 + 3	5 + 5
5 + 5	2 + 4	5 + 5	4 + 6	6 + 3
5 + 5	3 + 3	4 + 6	2 + 3	5 + 5

Name _____

9 + 0	5 + 5	3 + 4	7 + 3	4 + 4
2 + 2	3 + 5	1 + 9	2 + 3	2 + 7
6 + 3	2 + 5	3 + 7	6 + 2	2 + 8
6 + 4	1 + 6	4 + 5	3 + 3	0 + 5
7 + 2	3 + 6	5 + 2	2 + 4	4 + 6
4 + 3	5 + 3	8 + 2	5 + 4	2 + 6

Answer Key
Level A Addition

Page one Pretest

8	9	10	8	7
6	4	9	7	10
8	10	4	5	9
10	6	9	7	10
9	8	7	9	10
8	10	10	9	7

Page two (0-Rule)

4	0	10	1	6
8	10	5	2	7
9	1	9	3	8
6	3	2	9	7
4	6	9	0	1
2	10	8	5	4

Page three (0-Rule)

9	1	4	0	6
7	10	8	2	5
2	8	5	10	4
1	10	4	1	0
9	3	1	9	8
3	7	6	9	2

Page four (1-Rule)

5	3	6	9	4
6	0	7	4	7
2	10	8	9	3
8	1	10	7	9
6	4	5	7	9
5	6	10	8	2

Page five (1-Rule)

2	10	6	5	8
3	9	2	8	10
4	5	6	3	9
6	7	5	4	9
9	8	7	10	1
4	7	7	0	4

Page six (2+2)

1	4	4	4	7
4	9	4	2	8
4	3	4	3	4
2	4	9	8	5
4	4	10	4	6
8	4	5	7	4

Page seven (2+2)

4	8	7	4	5
2	4	8	9	4
1	4	4	7	4
4	4	6	4	10
9	4	2	8	4
4	5	4	3	3

Page eight (2+3)

8	5	6	4	5
9	6	5	4	5
5	4	4	5	2
10	5	7	4	5
5	9	4	5	2
4	5	5	4	5

Page nine (2+3)

4	5	9	5	6
5	7	10	4	5
5	5	4	5	4
4	6	5	8	5
5	4	4	5	2
2	4	5	9	5

Page ten (2+4)

4	6	3	6	2
6	5	4	6	6
4	6	6	5	6
6	9	6	9	5
1	6	5	6	4
6	5	4	3	6

Page eleven (2+4)

6	4	6	6	5
6	6	4	6	5
6	4	5	1	6
4	6	3	2	6
6	4	3	6	5
9	5	6	9	6

Page twelve (2+5)

7	8	6	7	5
6	7	10	4	7
7	5	5	7	6
6	7	8	5	7
7	4	6	7	0
7	7	4	6	7

Page thirteen (2+5)

5	5	7	6	7
7	0	4	7	6
8	7	5	7	6
7	7	7	6	4
10	7	4	6	7
7	8	6	7	5

Page fourteen (2+6)

6	8	7	8	5
8	3	6	7	8
5	8	1	8	6
8	4	8	5	7
6	8	7	4	8
8	9	8	6	7

Page fifteen (2+6)

8	7	8	4	5
5	8	7	8	6
7	6	8	9	8
8	1	5	8	1
7	8	6	3	8
8	4	7	8	6

Answer Key
Level A Addition

Page sixteen (2+7)

9	9	7	9	9
9	7	9	6	8
8	9	7	9	5
4	5	9	8	9
9	8	6	9	4
5	9	4	8	9

Page seventeen (2+7)

9	8	6	4	9
9	9	9	9	7
9	4	9	5	8
4	9	8	5	9
8	9	7	9	6
5	7	9	8	9

Page eighteen (2+8)

9	10	9	6	10
7	6	10	8	9
10	9	10	7	10
9	10	6	10	9
10	5	10	5	10
10	10	4	9	8

Page nineteen (2+8)

10	8	10	4	9
10	7	10	9	10
6	10	9	10	9
10	5	10	5	10
8	9	6	10	7
10	6	9	9	10

Page twenty (3+3)

8	6	7	6	10
6	5	9	9	6
6	10	6	4	6
6	6	8	6	10
6	10	6	10	9
10	6	9	7	6

Page twenty-one (3+3)

6	7	6	8	10
9	7	6	10	6
4	6	10	6	6
6	10	6	6	8
9	6	9	5	6
6	10	9	6	10

Page twenty-two (3+4)

10	7	6	5	7
7	6	8	7	6
9	10	7	7	7
6	7	7	7	9
7	4	7	6	8
6	7	9	6	7

Page twenty-three (3+4)

7	8	6	6	7
5	6	7	10	7
7	9	6	7	6
10	7	7	9	7
7	8	4	7	6
7	7	6	7	9

Page twenty-four (3+5)

8	8	10	8	7
5	8	7	7	8
8	4	9	8	9
6	8	7	7	8
8	6	7	7	8
8	6	8	10	7

Page twenty-five (3+5)

9	8	4	8	9
8	7	8	7	5
5	7	8	6	8
8	10	7	8	8
7	8	6	7	8
10	8	6	8	7

Page twenty-six (3+6)

6	9	7	7	9
9	4	9	8	8
8	9	5	9	10
9	9	8	7	9
4	9	9	3	8
9	8	10	9	6

Page twenty-seven (3+6)

8	9	9	7	9
6	9	10	9	8
9	7	9	7	6
9	3	4	8	9
4	9	8	8	9
9	5	10	9	8

Page twenty-eight (3+7)

9	4	10	6	10
10	5	8	10	8
10	10	7	9	10
10	9	9	10	6
7	10	9	9	10
10	7	10	6	9

Page twenty-nine (3+7)

9	10	7	10	9
10	4	9	6	10
6	7	10	9	10
5	10	8	10	8
10	6	9	10	9
10	10	7	9	10

Page thirty (4+4)

8	9	7	8	10
5	8	8	4	8
8	5	10	8	7
10	8	9	10	8
8	6	8	10	7
6	8	8	8	10

FS-23241 One-Minute Math Level A Addition

2 + 5	4 + 2	2 + 3	2 + 2	1 + 9	8 + 1
5 + 3	3 + 4	3 + 3	8 + 2	2 + 7	6 + 2
5 + 5	6 + 4	4 + 5	4 + 4	7 + 3	3 + 6

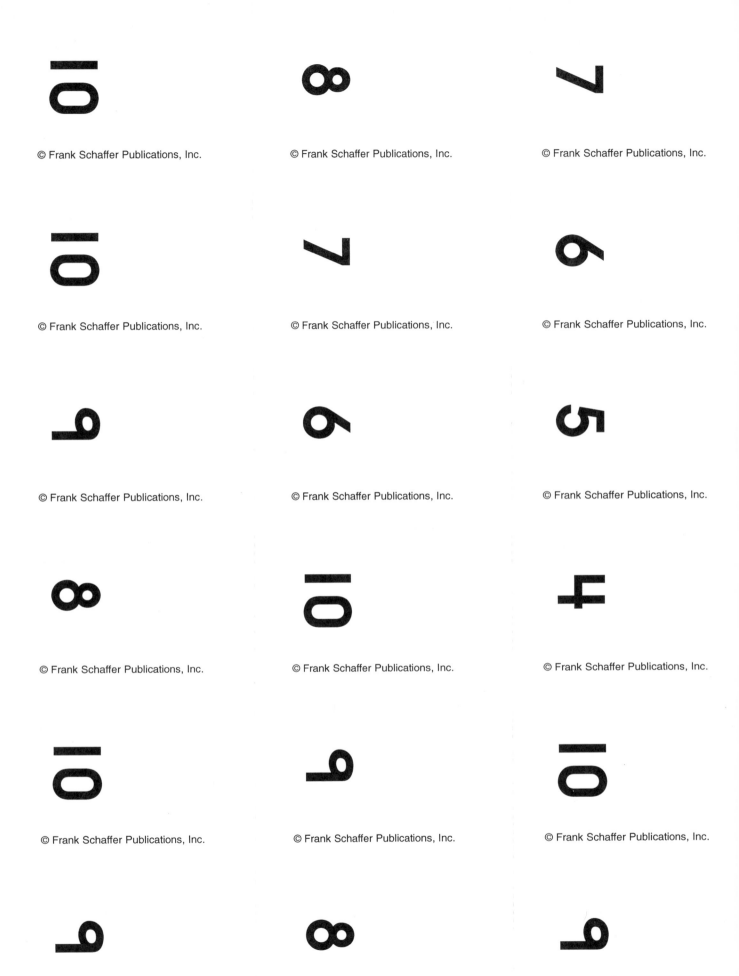

10

8

7

10

7

6

9

6

5

8

10

4

10

9

10

9

8

9

0 + 5	1 + 1	1 + 7
4 + 0	10 + 0	6 + 1
0 + 3	0 + 9	1 + 5
2 + 0	8 + 0	4 + 1
0 + 1	0 + 7	1 + 3
0 + 0	6 + 0	2 + 1

8

2

5

7

10

4

6

9

3

5

8

2

4

7

1

3

6

0